The artwork you'll encounter in this study is a unique creation by one of our talented youth students, Caroline Teel. Her illustrations offer a fresh perspective on the narrative, inviting you to see the story of Jonah in a new light.

All scriptures are noted in the New King James Version unless otherwise noted. The Holy Bible: New King James Version. (1982). Thomas Nelson. NB: 1982 is the original publication date and the date of this edition of the NKJV.

Introduction

What do you think about when you think of the story of Jonah?

Most people think of a giant fish or a whale when they reflect on the story of Jonah, although only 3 verses of Jonah's story are dedicated to that detail. Contrary to popular belief, the story of Jonah is more about God and his plans for a city than about the prophet Jonah. Through this narrative, we will see the failures of Jonah and God's relentless grace in the face of those failures.

3 Ways to Learn

- **Explanation** - Learning through receiving *step-by-step instructions* on how to do something. This type of learning is wonderful when it is available! When I had my first child, Brailey, I was terrified when they sent me home from the hospital with this fragile new baby. I was entrusted to care for, nurture, and raise her. I was terrified. All the books I read explaining what the coming days, months, and years would hold couldn't sufficiently prepare me for all I would face. That said, an explanation is sometimes insufficient even at its best.

- **Example** - Learning through the *experiences of others*. One of the reasons there are stories in the Bible is for us to see an example of things to do and not do. Additionally, stories help us see the consequences and rewards of our relationship with God.

- **Experience** - Learning through *our own experience*. Experience is a proven teacher, however, there's not enough time on this earth to have all the experiences needed to accumulate all the knowledge we need to thrive. Success is always our preferred source of learning, but failure has rich nutrients to receive from as well. Jonah's story is unique to the other Prophets because we learn from his failures rather than his words.

The goal of this study is to help you better understand the story of Jonah. However, during our time together, we will look at the overall narrative of scripture, and accumulate tools to help you better understand your whole Bible moving forward!

PART ONE
Man runs from God

Notes

Jonah 2:7 — When my soul fainted within me, I remembered the Lord; And my prayer went up to You, Into Your holy temple.

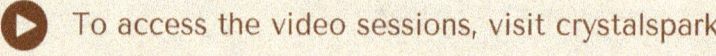 To access the video sessions, visit crystalsparks.org/jonah

Notes

 To access the video sessions, visit crystalsparks.org/jonah

Notes

 To access the video sessions, visit crystalsparks.org/jonah

Day One

CHALLENGE:
Read the book of Jonah in its entirety as we begin and highlight every time God is mentioned in the four chapters.

> How many times was God mentioned in the four chapters?
>
> _____
>
> How many times did we see God speaking?
>
> _____

As we begin our study, we need to identify the main character of the story. Despite what some might believe, the book of Jonah is more about God than it is about Jonah! Throughout this study, we will discover that Jonah got out of alignment with God's will when he started to believe that he was the main character of the story instead of God.

In the same way, God should be the main character in each of our own stories, and our stories don't make sense until we realize that Jesus is at the center instead of ourselves. Often we think of ourselves as the main character, and God is just a small part of the narrative.

Reflect on areas where you've made God the "supporting character" of your story instead of the one who calls the shots.

Day Two

> "Arise, go to Nineveh, that great city, and cry out against it; for their wickedness has come up before Me."
> **Jonah 1:2**

You have probably seen a child at some point who believed that as long as they couldn't see you they were invisible. Their visibility was ignorantly dependent on their own ability. My kids used to do something similar where they thought if they covered their eyes, they would be exempt from the punishment for their actions. They couldn't be punished as long as they couldn't see me!

Often, we carry this idea into our adult lives with God. People say things like, "I can't go to church the roof will fall in on me." This statement essentially says, "God only sees the sinfulness of my heart if I go to church." Their solution is to avoid God so they can't be held accountable for their behavior. The reality is that nothing is hidden from God. His watchful eye is on everything we do and every moment of our lives.

Let's look at some scriptures to see how God is keenly aware of every detail of our lives.

VERSE	WHAT DOES GOD OBSERVE?
Genesis 5:5	
1 Kings 9:2-4	
Acts 10:3-4	
Luke 5:22	

The beginning of the Book of Jonah shows us that nothing is hidden from God's watchful eye. As we continue, we will see that Jonah's heart is not exempt from God's observation either. It takes only one verse for us to see Jonah's rebellious heart on display.

Day Three

Let's continue to look at the themes in the book of Jonah. Consider the word "*great*."

When you think of the word "*great*" what do you think of? (List your initial thoughts on the word.)

_____

_____

_____

Let's look at some times "*great*" is used in the Bible:

VERSE	WHAT IS BEING CALLED GREAT?
Psalm 18:50	
Proverbs 26:10	
Ephesians 2:4-5	
Exodus 14:31	

The word "*great*" is used 8 times in the book of Jonah. Let's look at the ways it is used and what is being called great each time it is used.

VERSE	WHAT IS BEING CALLED GREAT?
Jonah 1:2	
Jonah 1:4	
Jonah 1:12	
Jonah 1:17	
Jonah 3:2	
Jonah 3:3	
Jonah 3:5	
Jonah 4:11	

Observe

Did you notice that there is only one chapter in Jonah that doesn't mention the word "great"?

Why does that chapter not mention the word "great"?
(Hint: Look at the chapter title to see what it focuses on)

_____

_____

_____

The most important One for us to see as great is God. It is so easy to exalt everything else in our lives and situations but fail to see the magnificence of our great God!

> Oh, magnify the Lord with me,
> And let us exalt His name together.
> **Psalm 34:3**

Who is the Psalmist asking us to magnify?

_____

_____

What does it look like to magnify the Lord practically?

_____

_____

_____

_____

Day Four

I once heard the statement, "God is preparing you for what He has prepared for you," and it changed my perspective on seasons of waiting. The things we get the most frustrated with are often the most effective at preparing us for what we will encounter in the future.

Look up the definition for "prepare" and write it below:

Let's look at the following verses from the book of Jonah and write down what was being prepared and who was preparing it.

VERSE	WHAT WAS PREPARED?	WHO PREPARED IT?
Jonah 1:17-2:1		
Jonah 4:6		
Jonah 4:7		
Jonah 4:8		

God was preparing Jonah with each item he prepared throughout the narrative. God used things in nature in an attempt to make Jonah into who he was called to be.

Keep the definition of "prepare" in mind as we look at the scriptures below. As you fill out the chart below, you will begin to clearly see what God was doing each step of the way to prepare Jonah.

VERSE	WHAT WAS GOD WANTING TO DO IN JONAH?
Jonah 1:17-2:1	
Jonah 4:6	
Jonah 4:7	
Jonah 4:8	

It's easy to point the finger at Jonah and forget that we are also being put through process to allow God to soften our hearts. Nineveh wasn't just a city for Jonah to visit. God wanted Jonah to see their repentant hearts, and for Jonah to become repentant too. God was more concerned with Jonah's heart than he was about his travel plans.

Just as God was after Jonah's heart, He is after yours! During our lives, we will come into contact with things that we cannot change. During those times of uncertainty, God begins to form us into who we are called to be.

Response

Take a moment and make your own chart of things that have happened in your life.

- **Circumstance:** Name a circumstance or experience that was beyond your control.
- **Heart Transformation:** What was the heart transformation God was after through it? Did you allow yourself to let God in or did you resist like Jonah? Take time to journal about it.
- **Prayer:** Write a prayer of thanksgiving or repentance around that circumstance.

CIRCUMSTANCE	HEART TRANSFORMATION	PRAYER
Trouble paying our bills.	I see now that you wanted me to rely on you as my provider for all my needs. I often attempt to be self-sufficient and not ask you first for what I need.	God, I repent for relying on my own ability to provide for myself. Help me to trust you to be my provider in all things. I want you to prepare me for what you have prepared for me.

JONAH 18

Day Five

Everyone reacts to difficulty in different ways. Some people will panic, others will weep, and some will take action to save themselves. In the passage below, everyone, including Jonah, reacts to the storm differently.

> Then the mariners were afraid; and every man cried out to his god, and threw the cargo that was in the ship into the sea, to lighten the load. But Jonah had gone down into the lowest parts of the ship, had lain down, and was fast asleep.
> **Jonah 1:5**

According to this verse, what was the mariners' reaction to the storm?

_____

_____

According to this verse, what was Jonah's reaction to the storm?

_____

_____

The sailors are running around the ship completely fearful, throwing cargo overboard, and most importantly - praying!

JONAH 19

In this verse, God is showing the passivity that had gripped Jonah's heart. Jonah not only lost compassion for the people of Nineveh, but he completely lacked any care for the mariners' lives as well. His hard heart caused him to fall asleep both naturally and spiritually.

The captain of the ship awakens Jonah and his speech parallels God's voice at the beginning of the story when they both address him with "arise." God uses a pagan ship captain to remind Jonah that the lives of people are dependent upon his obedience to the words of God.

	SIMILARITIES	DIFFERENCES
Jonah 1:1-2		
Jonah 1:6-7		

In both accounts, Jonah is told to "arise", "go," and he responds in disobedience. Our obedience impacts the lives of those around us.

PART TWO
Man runs to God

Notes

Psalm 135:6 — Whatever the Lord pleases He does, In heaven and in earth, In the seas and in all deep places.

To access the video sessions, visit crystalsparks.org/jonah

Notes

 To access the video sessions, visit crystalsparks.org/jonah

Notes

 To access the video sessions, visit crystalsparks.org/jonah

Day Six

To begin today's study, take a few moments to self-reflect on this question: "Who are you?" Write down some of your thoughts.

_____

_____

_____

> Then they said to him, "Please tell us! For whose cause is this trouble upon us? What is your occupation? And where do you come from? What is your country? And of what people are you?" So he said to them, "I am a Hebrew; and I fear the Lord, the God of heaven, who made the sea and the dry land."
> **Jonah 1:8-9**

What information did the mariners ask Jonah for?

1.
2.
3.
4.

How did Jonah answer?

1.
2.

Notice that Jonah primarily defined himself as a Hebrew. This is also the first identifier that culture would have placed on him as well. It is so easy to allow culture to define us instead of getting our identity from our Creator God.

VERSE	GOD'S WORD TELLS ME
John 1:12	
2 Corinthians 5:17	
John 15:15	
Jeremiah 1:9	

 Refuse to allow the world to define you differently than God's Word.

Jonah doesn't even mention his occupation although they ask him what it is. He is so resistant to God's call on his life to be a prophet to Nineveh that he isn't even willing to say it out loud! He was running from God even while his feet remained still.

Using what you have learned so far, how do you think God would have answered the mariner's four questions for Jonah?

1.
2.
3.
4.

Response

Now that we have considered Jonah, let's apply it to our own lives.

1 Why do difficult things happen in my life?

| 2 | Who does God say you are? |

| 3 | What are you called by God to do? |

Day Seven

> Now the Lord had prepared a great fish to swallow Jonah. And Jonah was in the belly of the fish three days and three nights.
> **Jonah 1:17**

Jonah took one of the most unique and infamous detours in history! He didn't want to be a part of God's plan so he ran as far away as he could. I doubt he could foresee this outcome when he diverted from God's original direction! The belly of a fish was the last consequence he could have imagined.

Ultimately, our sins will take us places we never wanted to go. When we choose to run from God, we end up in places much more uncomfortable than the place God intended to take us to. Running from God will always cost us!

3 Ways Running Costed Jonah

Financially
In Jonah 1:3, Jonah had to pay his fare to get as far away from where God was. In contrast, in Jonah 3:3 when he obeys, it costs him nothing to walk to where God asked him to go.

Physically
Nineveh was only 550 miles away from where our story began with Jonah. He paid the fare to take a boat to Tarshish which was 2500 miles away. At this time, this was the furthest you could travel in a day! Jonah thought if he distanced himself from where God was calling him, God would change His mind.

Relationally
Innocent people were put in harm's way on the boat because of Jonah's rebellion. Jonah's sinful acts didn't just impact himself but the lives of people around him. Our disobedience impacts us and those in our lives in more ways than we realize.

After reflecting on Jonah's story, how have your sins impacted your life financially, physically, or relationally?

_____

_____

_____

_____

_____

Remember: there is no sin that God can't forgive. There is no time that God can't redeem. God is a loving Father who is waiting for us to confess our sins so that He can forgive us and help us to live differently.

Response

- Read 1 John 1:9
- Write a prayer of repentance for your own life and ask God to help you live differently.

Day Eight

One way God helps move someone into reflective evaluation of themselves is through isolation. Isolation is one of the most effective ways to mature a leader and help someone learn who they are beyond what they have accomplished. Several times in a leader's lifetime, the leader may be set aside from normal ministry so that God can get their attention.

Isolation Process

Isolation Type	Lessons Observed
Bottom of the Ship	Jonah ran from God's call on his life and now finds himself at the bottom of the ship. Here he is aware that it is his fault that they are in the storm, but he is unwilling to come to a place of surrender. Instead, he waits for the mariners to take the action he should have been responsible for.
Belly of the Fish	Jonah finds himself inside the belly of the fish and God wants him to surrender to what is His plan. The fish surrenders Jonah to the very shore where the people live that he is called by God to serve. Jonah's heart is still not fully surrendered to God's plan.
Under the Tree	After the city comes to repentance, Jonah is upset and goes back into isolation. Here the Lord plants a tree for Jonah to find shelter, and Jonah's heart remains unsurrendered to God's plan. The tree surrenders to God's ultimate plan and dies, leaving the story with Jonah unwilling to surrender.

Each time Jonah finds himself "under" something, he is refusing to be under the hand of God.

Reflect

As we finish today's study, reflect on a season of your life when you found yourself, like Jonah, in isolation. Take time to reflect on lessons you learned in that season and what God did inside of you during those times of isolation.

SEASON OF ISOLATION	WHAT DID YOU LEARN?	WHAT DID GOD DO INSIDE OF YOU?

Day Nine

In Jonah 1:17 it says that the fish *swallowed* Jonah. This verb, "swallow" isn't isolated to Jonah's story, but it is a theme throughout the Bible. Look at the following passages to see other examples of how it's used.

VERSE	WHO/WHAT WAS SWALLOWED?	WHY WERE THEY SWALLOWED?
EXODUS 7:8-13		
NUMBERS 16:1-2, 28-32		

In each of these scriptures, God was working out the details of a bigger, more ultimate plan than what they could see in front of them. In Exodus, God was making a way for His people to receive freedom from oppression. With Korah, God was trying to keep rebellion from the people so they could walk according to all that He called them to do. God always has people on his mind, and through each of these "swallow" stories, His ultimate plan was to save a group of people.

Observe

God is showing salvation through judgment in each of these "swallow" stories.

- Jonah being swallowed by the fish is God's judgment for the rebellion in Jonah's heart.
- The fish is also a picture of salvation for Jonah, as it serves as a place for his rescue.

Now that we have looked at what happens when "swallow" is mentioned in scripture, let's refer back to Jonah's story and apply what we've learned.

Response

Why was Jonah swallowed?

_____

_____

Who does God have on His mind when Jonah was swallowed?

_____

_____

Day Ten

> Now the Lord had prepared a great fish to swallow Jonah. And Jonah was in the belly of the fish three days and three nights.
> **Jonah 1:17**

Today we are going to look at the theme of "three days" in the Bible. Often when we see "three days" mentioned in the Bible, it carries a pattern of going from death to life. The most common example of this is Jesus' death and resurrection! The original audience of Jonah would have thought of some of the following stories when hearing this theme again of "three nights" in Jonah 1:17.

VERSE	WHAT IS LACKING?	WHAT HAPPENS NEXT?
Exodus 15:22-25		
Genesis 22:4-13		
2 Kings 20:1-6		
Hosea 6:1-2		

When "three days" is mentioned in the context of Jonah, it helps us to see that God's heart is to bring Jonah from death to life. Ultimately, He desires to bring us from our spiritual death to eternal life in the same way.

Human beings can't live inside of a fish without some sort of supernatural assistance. God sustains Jonah in a place where he would never be able to fulfill His great rescue plan for a city.

Reflect

Take a moment to reflect on how God has brought *you* from death to life. All of us have been rescued by Jesus Christ. I had a debt that I could not pay, and Jesus paid a debt He did not owe.

> But God, who is rich in mercy, because of His great love with which He loved us, even when we were dead in trespasses, made us alive together with Christ (by grace you have been saved), and raised us up together, and made us sit together in the heavenly places in Christ Jesus, that in the ages to come He might show the exceeding riches of His grace in His kindness toward us in Christ Jesus.
> **Ephesians 2:4-7**

According to the verse above, what were you dead in?

_____

_____

Look up the definition of "trespass" and write it below:

Define	TRESPASS

According to the previous passage in Ephesians, where are you now seated?

_____

Just as Jonah could not live on the inside of a fish without divine assistance, we could not access heavenly places without Christ dying for us and making us alive in Him. God gives us access to what was formerly inaccessible by His Spirit.

PART THREE
Man runs with God

Notes

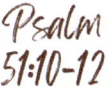
Create in me a clean heart, O God, And renew a steadfast spirit within me. Do not cast me away from Your presence, And do not take Your Holy Spirit from me. Restore to me the joy of Your salvation, And uphold me by Your generous Spirit.

 To access the video sessions, visit crystalsparks.org/jonah

Notes

 To access the video sessions, visit crystalsparks.org/jonah

Notes

 To access the video sessions, visit crystalsparks.org/jonah

Day Eleven

Today we are going to focus on Jonah's prayer in chapter two. Before we begin, look at the scriptures below and see if you can recognize their common theme.

> I acknowledged my sin to You, and my iniquity I have not hidden. I said, "I will confess my transgressions to the Lord," and You forgave the iniquity of my sin. Selah
> **Psalm 32:5**

> Have mercy upon me, O God, According to Your lovingkindness; according to the multitude of Your tender mercies, blot out my transgressions. Wash me thoroughly from my iniquity, and cleanse me from my sin. For I acknowledge my transgressions, and my sin is always before me. Against You, You only, have I sinned, And done this evil in Your sight— that You may be found just when You speak, and blameless when You judge.
> **Psalm 51:1-4**

What is the common theme you see within these prayers?

_____

_____

Jonah Two

1 Then Jonah prayed to the Lord his God from the fish's belly.
2 And he said:
"I cried out to the Lord because of my affliction,
And He answered me.
"Out of the belly of Sheol I cried,
And You heard my voice.
3 For You cast me into the deep,
Into the heart of the seas,
And the floods surrounded me;
All Your billows and Your waves passed over me.
4 Then I said, 'I have been cast out of Your sight;
Yet I will look again toward Your holy temple.'
5 The waters surrounded me, *even* to my soul;
The deep closed around me;
Weeds were wrapped around my head.
6 I went down to the moorings of the mountains;
The earth with its bars *closed* behind me forever;
Yet You have brought up my life from the pit,
O Lord, my God.
7 "When my soul fainted within me,
I remembered the Lord;
And my prayer went *up* to You,
Into Your holy temple.
8 "Those who regard worthless idols
Forsake their own Mercy.
9 But I will sacrifice to You
With the voice of thanksgiving;
I will pay what I have vowed.
Salvation *is* of the Lord."
10 So the Lord spoke to the fish, and it vomited Jonah onto dry *land*.

Follow these prompts as you read Jonah 2

1. 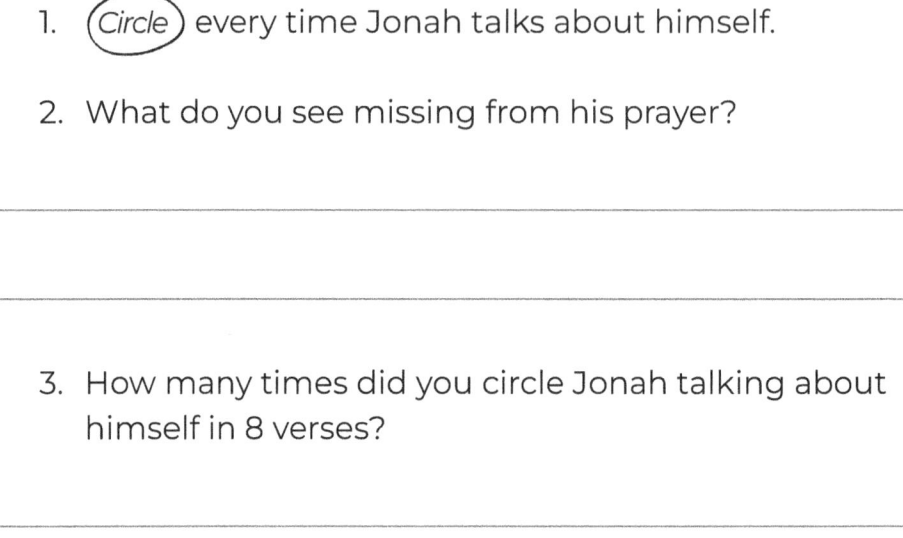 every time Jonah talks about himself.

2. What do you see missing from his prayer?

   _____

   _____

3. How many times did you circle Jonah talking about himself in 8 verses?

   _____

Reading Jonah's prayer we see Jonah's perspective is that God *only* does good things in response to *Jonah's* faithfulness. In reality, God does answer our prayers, however, the goodness we receive from God is *despite* us not *because* of us.

> But we are all like an unclean *thing,* And all our righteousnesses *are* like filthy rags; We all fade as a leaf, And our iniquities, like the wind, Have taken us away.
> **Isaiah 64:6**

According to this scripture, our righteousness is like a filthy rag. Everything God does in our lives is because *He* is good and faithful, not because we are. When we get the source of our righteousness confused we begin to think we *earn* God's goodness and we stop *receiving* God's goodness.

Day Twelve

Everything we are looking for is on the other side of our prayers. Often, the reason for our prayerless lives is because we believe in the lie that we can do the call of God without God. In reality, the opposite of that is true! Throughout scripture, the unimaginable happened when God's people began to pray and rely on God!

VERSE	RESULT OF PRAYER
James 5:17-18	
Acts 4:31	
Acts 9:39-41	
1 Samuel 1:9-11, 20	
Isaiah 38:1-6	

Each of these passages contains beautiful stories of answered prayer! Sometimes our answer to prayer is anything less than beautiful but it is exactly what we need in that season from God!

> So the Lord spoke to the fish, and it vomited Jonah onto dry land.
> **Jonah 2:10**

What was the result of Jonah's prayer?

_____

_____

Imagine what that moment was like for Jonah. What do you think it looked, smelled, and felt like? Take a moment to write down what you imagine.

_____

_____

_____

Why do you think it happened in that way?

_____

_____

Now, think about your life. Are there areas of your life that look, smell, and feel like fish vomit but in reality they are God's goodness in your life?

JONAH 48

It's really easy to focus on the unpleasant aspects of our circumstances rather than reflect on God's grace that is present in those same moments. If we are honest with ourselves, we have all been like Jonah. We have all had moments when our disobedience has landed us in situations that should have been the end of us, but when we cried out to God we were delivered!

The remnant of the unpleasant circumstances will always be present in our deliverance. Practically, it might look like living on a budget because of the previous lack of responsibility for our finances, or marriage counseling to undo the wounds we inflicted on our spouse because of our selfishness. Fish vomit doesn't seem like a beautiful answer to prayer but it was for Jonah. Jonah should have died in the sea, but God spared His life. Even more so, he transported him to the shore to have a second chance.

Take a moment to reflect on your own life and see how some of the unpleasant circumstances you've gone through had answers to prayer weaved within them.

UNPLEASANT CIRCUMSTANCE	HOW WAS IT AN ANSWER TO PRAYER?

Day Thirteen

We all want a second chance when we've made a mistake! An opportunity to start over, to redeem ourselves, to correct what's been done wrong.

Interestingly, Jonah chapter 3 begins the same way as chapter 1 began. In fact, the first 9 words of each chapter are exactly the same. This is important because it helps us see that God is giving Jonah a second chance. He calls him again, with the opportunity to obey rather than run. Although they are similar, there are still differences to observe. Take time to read the following passages and write down what you observe.

VERSE	SIMILARITIES	DIFFERENCES
Jonah 1:1-3		
Jonah 3:1-3		

Reflect on the similarities in these two passages. Why do they matter to the story of Jonah?

_____

_____

Reflect on the differences in these two passages. Why do they matter to the story of Jonah?

_____

_____

Today, I want you to think about the second chances God has given you. Scripture doesn't record if Jonah said anything to God in response to his second chance. Write your heart response to the second chances God has given you along the way.

Pray — WRITE A PRAYER OF THANKSGIVING FOR SECOND CHANCES

Day Fourteen

> Now the word of the Lord came to Jonah the second time, saying, 2 "Arise, go to Nineveh, that great city, and preach to it the message that I tell you." 3 So Jonah arose and went to Nineveh, according to the word of the Lord. Now Nineveh was an exceedingly great city, a three-day journey in extent.
> **Jonah 3:1-3**

Nothing is better than second chances. The biggest second chance we can receive is one at life! A woman in our church received a bleak diagnosis from the doctor, but she believed God for a miracle and that she would not just survive but thrive. God answered her prayer and she is completely healed today! Shortly after she received her miracle she shared how her entire outlook on life has shifted. She began to take the trips she used to only dream about. She invested time with family instead of prioritizing work. She lives every day with the sober awareness that she should have died, but now she has been gifted a second chance at life.

This is such a beautiful illustration of second chances, but it's not isolated to her medical breakthrough. You too were sentenced to death for your sins, but you were given a second chance at life because of Christ's sacrifice.

And you, being dead in your trespasses and the uncircumcision of your flesh, He has made alive together with Him, having forgiven you all trespasses,
Colossians 2:13

What were you dead in?

How are you made alive?

This verse is similar to the verse we looked at on day ten (Ephesians 2:4-7). We were all dead and without hope, until God gave us a second chance at life through His Son, Jesus.

The life you are living is a second chance given by the grace of God. For Jonah, when given a second chance he obeyed what God was asking him to do instead of choosing to run away!

Reflect

Is there anything in your life you need to change?

Are there areas of your life where you are resisting God's commands?

Gratitude Practice

- **Read** Lamentations 3:21-23
- **Reflect** on the second, third, or one hundredth chance God has given to you.
- **Allow gratitude** to flood your heart for His grace extended to you.
- **Write** what you're grateful for below.

Day Fifteen

And Jonah began to enter the city on the first day's walk. Then he cried out and said, "Yet forty days, and Nineveh shall be overthrown!" So the people of Nineveh believed God, proclaimed a fast, and put on sackcloth, from the greatest to the least of them. Then word came to the king of Nineveh; and he arose from his throne and laid aside his robe, covered himself with sackcloth and sat in ashes. And he caused it to be proclaimed and published throughout Nineveh by the decree of the king and his nobles, saying, let neither man nor beast, herd nor flock, taste anything; do not let them eat, or drink water. But let man and beast be covered with sackcloth, and cry mightily to God; yes, let every one turn from his evil way and from the violence that is in his hands. Who can tell if God will turn and relent, and turn away from His fierce anger, so that we may not perish? Then God saw their works, that they turned from their evil way; and God relented from the disaster that He had said He would bring upon them, and He did not do it.
Jonah 3:4-10

 every time sackcloth is mentioned in the above passage.

 who is wearing the sackcloth.

We've spent considerable time looking at Jonah's prayer from chapter two. Now, look at Nineveh's repentance and compare it to Jonah's lack of genuine repentance in chapter two.

Unlike Jonah, the people of Nineveh wore sackcloth as a sign of their repentance (Jonah 3:5,6,8). Even the animals in Nineveh were noted as wearing sackcloth! Imagine driving by a field and seeing all of the cows in sackcloth clothing. No one was exempt from responding to God's message through the prophet Jonah. This is a revival of epic proportions!

In Jonah 3:9, we see the king was hopeful that God would show mercy to his people. Contrarily, Jonah made no mention of the possibility of mercy in his captivating sermon in Jonah 3:4. There was a supernatural faith in the heart of the king that hoped for God to reverse the judgment that was due them. In turn, the entire nation repented. No social class, people, or animal was exempt. To better understand the significance of sackcloth and ashes, look at a few other times this concept is used in scripture in the context of repentance.

VERSE	WHO WAS WEARING SACKCLOTH?	WHAT WAS IT FOR?
ESTHER 4:1-4		
NEHEMIAH 9:1-3		
DANIEL 9:3-5		

As you saw in the previous exercise, there are plenty of examples of God's people wearing sackcloth and repenting. But in Jonah 3, it's the *sinful* city of Nineveh wearing sackcloth and repenting.

Sackcloth and ashes were an outward sign of what God was doing inwardly within their hearts. In the New Testament, we don't see sackcloth and ashes, but there are still outward signs of inward changes God is doing in our lives. Let's look at some and as you read the scriptures write your observations.

VERSE	WHAT WAS THE OUTWARD SIGN OF AN INWARD CHANGE?
Acts 2:37-38	
Acts 8:35-38	
Acts 9:17-18	

Repentance is beautiful to the Lord. In fact, it is irresistible to Him!

Read Jonah 3:9-10 and list out the things that stand out to you about God's actions.

_____

_____

_____

_____

Imagine how foolish it felt to make clothing for the animals. I have found when we are walking in true repentance, it will often look foolish to the world around us.

JONAH 58

Are there areas in your life where God wants you to walk in repentance but you are fearful of what people will think of you?

PART FOUR
Man runs against God

Notes

Matthew 6:14-15 For if you forgive men their trespasses, your heavenly Father will also forgive you. But if you do not forgive men their trespasses, neither will your Father forgive your trespasses.

 To access the video sessions, visit crystalsparks.org/jonah

Notes

 To access the video sessions, visit crystalsparks.org/jonah

Notes

 To access the video sessions, visit crystalsparks.org/jonah

Day Sixteen

When the word of the Lord first came to Jonah he had a much different response than that of the king of Nineveh. I want you to look at the two portions of scripture and see the similarities and differences.

	SIMILARITIES	DIFFERENCES
Jonah 1:1-3		
Jonah 3:6-7		

Jonah was a great prophet who had witnessed God doing amazing miracles. He knew God intimately and had been used by God before (2 Kings 14:23-27). Unfortunately, sometimes our knowledge of God keeps us from obeying Him fully.

Contrarily, the sinful king and people of Nineveh approached the Lord with such tenderness. They have such a different response to hearing the word of the Lord.

Look at the following scriptures and how they responded to God.

	HOW MUCH KNOWLEDGE DID THEY HAVE?	WHAT WAS THE RESULT?
Matthew 23:27-28		
Luke 8:43-48		
Matthew 4:18-22		

Often, we think that if we knew more about God we could really obey Him. That simply isn't true. It isn't your knowledge about God that is keeping you from living the life God wants for you, but the position of your heart.

Throughout scripture, God mostly used people whose hearts were yielded to His Word. They didn't need an explanation or a logical discourse to convince them to obey God, they simply allowed God to do whatever He wanted in their lives.

Reflect

What stood out the most to you from today's study?

What has God asked you to do?

Day Seventeen

The overarching theme of Jonah is the lost people being found.

- The mariners knew they were lost and woke Jonah in search of assistance.
- The people of Nineveh were lost, and they knew they couldn't defend their sinful ways when confronted with God's Word.

Each of them took action when they had a revelation of their sin and separation from God. The mariners made sacrifices to God in Jonah 1:16. In Jonah 3:7, the people of Nineveh began fasting and praying.

In the midst of all of this, we see Jonah building a home for himself to be comfortable as he waits for the destruction of the people he hates (Jonah 4:5). The only person in the story who doesn't know they are lost and in need of help is Jonah.

> For the Son of Man has come to seek and to save that which was lost.
> **Luke 19:10**

What did Jesus come to do?

Luke 19:10 tells us that Jesus was *seeking* us. A lot of times our salvation story is about how we found Jesus, but in actuality, He was the one seeking us.

The way He seeks us doesn't stop at salvation. He continually looks for us throughout our entire lives. Who looks for people in a tree? Jesus does when he looks for Zaccheaus in Luke 19:1-5. Who would think of looking in a cemetery for someone that society has discarded? Jesus does in Luke 8:26-38 when He heals the demon-possessed man.

How hard are you to find?

Jesus didn't come just to seek the lost, but to *save* the lost! Sometimes we wonder what God wants to do on the earth today, but the answer is clear. He wants to save lost people.

Who do you know that is lost?

God's desire was for Jonah to go to the lost people of Nineveh and give them an opportunity to be saved. We too have received a commissioning to the lost in the following passage of scripture.

> And Jesus came and spoke to them, saying, "All authority has been given to Me in heaven and on earth. Go therefore and make disciples of all the nations, baptizing them in the name of the Father and of the Son and of the Holy Spirit, teaching them to observe all things that I have commanded you; and lo, I am with you always, *even* to the end of the age." Amen.
> **Matthew 28:18-20**

From Matthew 28:18-20, what actions are we commanded to do:

_____

_____

_____

What does that look like practically?

_____

_____

_____

There are no places exempt from God's Great Commission to us. He wants us to take the Gospel to the ends of the earth!

We often allow fear to keep us from spreading the Gospel, but the worst thing that could happen is to finish this study and your heart remain unchanged like Jonah. Jonah finally obeyed God at the end of the story, but his heart remained hard and resistant towards God.

Make the decision today to allow God to soften your heart and change your perspective of the world around you!

Day Eighteen

> But it displeased Jonah exceedingly, and he became angry. So he prayed to the Lord, and said, "Ah, Lord, was not this what I said when I was still in my country? Therefore I fled previously to Tarshish; for I know that You are a gracious and merciful God, slow to anger and abundant in lovingkindness, One who relents from doing harm. Therefore now, O Lord, please take my life from me, for it is better for me to die than to live!"
> **Jonah 4:1-3**

Imagine an entire city being saved at once! We don't know the exact number included in this city, but we know for certain there were at least 120,000 people saved that day (Jonah 4:11). What an incredible miracle for so many lives to be changed!

> I tell you that in the same way there will be more rejoicing in heaven over one sinner who repents than over ninety-nine righteous persons who do not need to repent.
> **Luke 15:7**

According to this verse, what is heaven's reaction when one person gets saved?

_____

_____

Jonah's reaction is very contrary to heaven's reaction in Luke 15.

Contrast Jonah's reaction in Jonah 4:1-3 with God's reaction in Luke 15:7. Reflect on the emotions Jonah had and notice how they differ from heaven's emotions.

JONAH'S REACTION (JONAH 4:1-3)	GOD'S REACTION (LUKE 15:7)

We are treading dangerous ground when we believe we are the only ones worthy of grace. In this heart posture, we begin to become resentful when God gives grace to people we don't like.

Unfortunately, we often want forgiveness for ourselves but justice for everyone else. A modern example of the heart of Jonah would be getting angry when the person you don't like at work gets promoted or becoming joyful when someone who hurt you goes through a devastating season. We may not build a house on a hill just to view their devastation like Jonah, but we scroll social media looking for signs of their misfortune.

The reality is that God has already forgiven the people that you are choosing not to forgive. You are the only one keeping a record of their wrongs. It's time to let go! Your bitterness is only poisoning you while the other person remains unscathed.

> For if you forgive men their trespasses, your heavenly Father will also forgive you. But if you do not forgive men their trespasses, neither will your Father forgive your trespasses.
> **Matthew 6:14-15**

According to this verse, when do I receive forgiveness?

_____

_____

_____

If you're honest with yourself, is there anyone you hope God won't forgive?

_____

_____

Resentment keeps us from seeing the faithfulness of God all around us. We become record keepers of wrongdoing rather than focused on what God is doing.

Write down all the ways God has been faithful to Jonah.

_____

_____

_____

_____

> Therefore be imitators of God as dear children.
> **Ephesians 5:1**

From exercise earlier today, do you see more of the characteristics of Jonah or God in yourself?

_____

_____

JONAH 73

How would Jonah's actions have changed if he had focused on God's actions rather than the wrongs of the people of Nineveh?

_____

_____

_____

_____

How would your life look different if you focused more on God's actions rather than the wrongs of others? Explain.

_____

_____

_____

_____

_____

Day Nineteen

So Jonah went out of the city and sat on the east side of the city. There he made himself a shelter and sat under it in the shade, till he might see what would become of the city. And the Lord God prepared a plant and made it come up over Jonah, that it might be shade for his head to deliver him from his misery. So Jonah was very grateful for the plant. But as morning dawned the next day God prepared a worm, and it so damaged the plant that it withered. And it happened, when the sun arose, that God prepared a vehement east wind; and the sun beat on Jonah's head, so that he grew faint. Then he wished death for himself, and said, "It is better for me to die than to live."

Then God said to Jonah, "Is it right for you to be angry about the plant?" And he said, "It is right for me to be angry, even to death!"

But the Lord said, "You have had pity on the plant for which you have not labored, nor made it grow, which came up in a night and perished in a night. And should I not pity Nineveh, that great city, in which are more than one hundred and twenty thousand persons who cannot discern between their right hand and their left—and much livestock?"
Jonah 4:5-11

Most of us have experienced an event in which your seat location really matters! No matter the cost, we don't want to come to an event and have a seat where we can't see properly the highly anticipated performance we came for. Jonah had this same point of view when he left the city and set up a temporary home on the hill where he could watch the city spiral into what he anticipated to be their demise. He was prepared with proverbial popcorn in hand to see God change His mind and destroy the city. We aren't told this explicitly in the text, but I think he would have stayed there as long as it took to see God destroy the people he despised.

Reflect

Think about just how much hate would have to reside in your heart to enjoy watching someone else's destruction. Why do you think Jonah hated Nineveh to this extent?

_____

_____

_____

_____

Read Jonah 2 - What did Jonah promise to do for God?

_____

_____

Jonah forgot so quickly all that he had promised God he would do. He realized in Jonah 2:9 that salvation belongs to the Lord, and it wasn't his decision to whom God extended grace! Now, he is awaiting the destruction of a city that God loved despite their failures and reputation.

It's easy to point out how Jonah did wrong without really evaluating our own lives and where we failed to do what God asked of us. We have all prayed desperately trying to get out of a difficult situation and made promises we didn't intend to keep. These prayers can sound like, "God if you get me out of this [insert really difficult situation] then I promise [insert big declaration of what we will do in return]." Oftentimes, God saves us and we forget the promise we made when the desperation has worn off.

Jonah didn't follow through with all that he promised God, but God still responded with grace. God continued to try to change Jonah's heart up to His final words. However, Jonah was so consumed with his own plan that he couldn't perceive God's plan.

In Jonah 4:8, God responds by sending a strong wind against Jonah, echoing how the story began (Jonah 1:4). Despite the journey Jonah has endured, his heart remains unchanged.

What did Jonah choose to pity in Jonah 4:9-10?

_____

_____

In what ways have you misplaced your pity or compassion? Name a situation where you've mourned for what's been lost and forgotten the bigger picture of what God was doing.

_____

_____

Jonah's story ends without any resolution of the fate of Jonah or the city of Nineveh. We are forced to ask ourselves questions and face our own heart postures that have been skewed. We must allow God to reveal the places where our hearts are misaligned with His.

Take a moment to pause and ask God if there are any areas where your heart is misaligned with His. Repent for allowing your heart to harden and allow Him to shape your heart to look like His.

AREA MY HEART IS MISALIGNED	PRAYER OF REPENTANCE

Day Twenty

Throughout all of scripture, we see the theme of man's brokenness and desperate need for a Savior. We know that ultimately, Jesus fulfills that need for humanity.

While it's easy to find Jesus in reading the New Testament, I want to challenge you to find him even in scripture where He isn't explicitly named. Our whole Bible points to humanity's need for Christ.

Jesus shows us the connection between Him and the prophet Jonah in the following scripture. He is attempting to open their eyes to see that He is an even better prophet than Jonah was.

> Then some of the scribes and Pharisees answered, saying, "Teacher, we want to see a sign from You."
> But He answered and said to them, "An evil and adulterous generation seeks after a sign, and no sign will be given to it except the sign of the prophet Jonah. For as Jonah was three days and three nights in the belly of the great fish, so will the Son of Man be three days and three nights in the heart of the earth.
> **Matthew 12:38-40**

JONAH	JESUS
Judgment for his sins	Judgment for the sins of the world
Jonah alive in a fish	Jesus alive on the throne
City saved	World saved
Received a Word from God for sinners	Word became flesh to redeem sinners
Sinful act brings the storm of God's judgment, bringing danger to sailors	Calms the storm and saves the sinners on the boat
Helpless against the wind and waves	Holds all authority over the wind and waves
Fled from God's will for his life	Submitted to God's will for His life

How has this study helped you see the gospel differently?

_____

_____

_____

_____

How has your understanding of Jonah's story changed?

What parts of Jonah's life convicted you personally?

I am so thankful that we got to do this study together! Thank you for going on the journey with me.

Notes

 To access the video sessions, visit crystalsparks.org/jonah

Notes

 To access the video sessions, visit crystalsparks.org/jonah

Notes

 To access the video sessions, visit crystalsparks.org/jonah

Notes

 To access the video sessions, visit crystalsparks.org/jonah

Notes

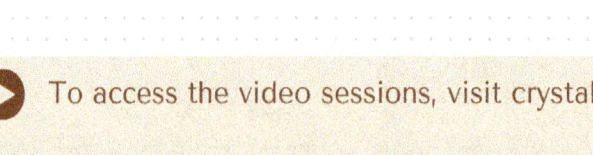
To access the video sessions, visit crystalsparks.org/jonah

Notes

 To access the video sessions, visit crystalsparks.org/jonah

About Crystal Sparks

Crystal Sparks is a writer, speaker, and pastor who is passionate about encouraging people to fulfill the dreams that God has placed in their heart. Raised in the small Texas town of Sulphur Springs, Crystal's life was profoundly transformed when she encountered God in the midst of her difficult teenage years.

In her 23 years of ministry, she has served in the role of Youth Pastor, Associate Pastor, and Lead Pastor. Crystal has spoken for various sports teams, youth events, church conferences, and women's gatherings both nationally and internationally. In 2014, she relocated with her husband Bryan and their two children, Brailey and Bear, to plant a life-giving church in Caddo Mills, Texas. Together, Crystal and Bryan serve as Lead Pastors of One Church.

WWW.CRYSTALSPARKS.ORG

www.ingramcontent.com/pod-product-compliance
Lightning Source LLC
Chambersburg PA
CBHW081354040426
42450CB00016B/3431